THE KEEP

T0108924

KUHL HOUSE POETS

edited by

Jorie Graham

&

Mark Levine

The Keep

poems by

EMILY WILSON

UNIVERSITY OF IOWA PRESS

Ψ IOWA CITY

University of Iowa Press, Iowa City 52242
Printed in the United States of America

Text design by Shari DeGraw

http://www.uiowa.edu/~uipress

The publication of this book was generously
supported by the University of Iowa Foundation.

Printed on acid-free paper

Library of Congress Cataloging-in-Publication Data
Wilson, Emily, 1968–
    The keep: poems / by Emily Wilson.
        p.   cm.—(Kuhl House poets)
    ISBN 0-87745-773-5 (pbk.)
        I. Title.   II. Series.
    PS3623.158 K44   2001
    811'.6—dc21
                                                    2001027431

01   02   03   04   05   P   5   4   3   2   1

For my family

CONTENTS

Acknowledgments   IX

° I °

Nonesuch   3
Hortus Siccus   4
Terra Nullius   5
Ars Botanica   6
The Fossil Garden   7
Pastoral   8
Relict   9
Green River   10
Notes from the Mesa   11
Landscape Primitive   12
Requiescat   13
Via Dolorosa   15
Legend   16

° II °

Radical Field   19

° III °

Winter Journal   35

° IV °

Ontogeny   55

° V °

The Keep   69
Geomantic   70
Eve Pieces   71
Slow Water Primer   84
Carnac   85

ACKNOWLEDGMENTS

Grateful acknowledgment to the editors of the journals in which some of these poems first appeared: *Explosive*: "Green River," "Relict," "Pastoral," "Requiescat" (as "Lines for Jimmy Nye"), "Geomantic"; *Kenning*: "Landscape Primitive"; *TriQuarterly*: from "Ontogeny": "In lilacs is reason gone," "Snow founders under," "Those thermal bursts," "I study you as you."

Many, many thanks to my teachers, my friends, and the Sargent Street regulars. Thank you, Kathy. Thank you, Mark.

∘ **I** ∘

NONESUCH

You come from unquiet
country into rooms

the marshes empty to
at low tide. Region

of seed kind. Its terraces
secreted in rivers.

The implicate system
you live in or that which is

all the while here unrenders
itself, a civility

of capture and let run.
You are wondrous

in a fundament of greens.
Unknown but you are.

HORTUS SICCUS

Now we get autumn

agricultural
ambuscades

between windfall

just so I know you

mean business

inordinate
to sleep through

the follicles

unzippering

when you've turned yourself
out I'll come to

perennial
paresthesias

the cosmos all

obviate

TERRA NULLIUS

No church utters up.
No rute-mark.

No roadhouse paroling
its ghosts.

A while since you spoke

toward the traffic.
Might I disturb you?

What is evidence here

of the sporophore?
What is known to be stringent

on the lung?
What is edible what

is insect what is
terminus?

So far to have come without fix.

To view the heirloom

everlastings.

ARS BOTANICA

To bear you in mind.

To be jammed in your saffrons.

The abasement of these ditches
of your smolderings.

Of your abasement.

Follow this in:

we go weatherward?
is this tenable?

The roothairs fuse
for the openings
to shoot from.

You leaf
on the potentate's dome?

You remnant
in need of finishing?

You gilt
and swift execution?

THE FOSSIL GARDEN

Some spare relief
of sedges so many

million years old.
As if articles

of faith were
unnumbered. As if

the seminal
mind could be prized

from its berth.
In the intricate

underworld birds
are abstracts of

collapse without ground.
You come to some end.

And love that season
travels hungry.

PASTORAL

The mordants in their noise,
the night transports.

A means of coming to
the switchyard of the tongue.

To have once
set such store by

forced creatures.
Not changed toward

something of my own.
The towns raised chaffed

seas to ground them.
In that frieze before

storm you went on.
Effigy loomed out

of cornfield. Future
inside its trussed forms.

RELICT

This is the ocean
dead-reckoned into

autumn estuarial
grounds in which drift

an aberrance of terns,
the few barrier

cottages closed up.
The small vowel-shifts

we have been through.
This trend toward hometowns

that are evermore
strange. The textures

eccentric in mud.
Not figuring your end.

You become the lone trove
of whole kingdoms.

GREEN RIVER

There is the mountain
that became the barren

of rudiment silt.
There is emergent

instinct that stalled,
acquainted then strayed

to what odds. Far
above the miniature

tamarisk-imperfect
shore the sediments

burn in their curtains.
You've taken so long

to come through.
The archival exit

speech still stayed
at the mouth.

NOTES FROM THE MESA

for Kate

Outbuildings refusing to come down.
Some little scavenger

polishing its tongue.
The pole fence going mindless

alongside us.
The road burnishes itself

down to a bottomwater.
How we have come to be here

among the other creatures —
backward.

Bees in the cabinetry
brushed out of their skeletons.

Someone's having troubled
after the ruined boots.

So the mountain just stands there
where we can witness

its face being scoured.
Like looking into a world scarcely handled.

LANDSCAPE PRIMITIVE

Nothing possessed me
but the ordinary

strain of distance
upon natural objects.

Black trees against
the matte of tableland.

Each creature in
its stead, the brute

particles reordered
to an unforgiving.

There was this
skeleton inside me.

I could not say where
I had been most of my life.

The glaciers hiss
like gods going under.

REQUIESCAT

for Jimmy Nye

You have left
the flickers to run
up their scripts
and the salt ponds
to the clonal reed
grass and the mink
to its circuits and
the house to its warps
and to its vitals.

Winter in its long
composition
of boxcars trundled
across bottomland.
Now is the stop-
yard of your intimate
and slack-tongued garden.

The mob of black earth
quells in spadesful.
I did not even know
you but still.

Old suit from its back-
drawer pins and the eye
in its shut hutch

but the hands
at their own
inscrutable
use to the heart.

VIA DOLOROSA

Channel wind laps in the foils
of scrub pines, figuring their keep.

I can only go this counterfeit way
into your factory lands, your paddocks.

All to learn a waiting man's wisdom,
how to steady at the instruments

for night. What urgence are the ruins
at Arromanches, those slow-molded, half-

submergible moons and the combs
of tidal verdigris you are come to.

LEGEND

for Wendell Wilson

Sometimes the river leaves
your name in logged tones,
how it saw you managing

the masts, stripping timbers,
stem and keel, pinning black
spruce rib to tamarack knee.

Your *Domain* was the risk
you would minister,
how she took to her first

dive like a waterborn,
a trick of the marsh reeds
blistering. The river says

you grew that day and the fine
shadows crept in behind
from the sheetwork before the sun.

The spirit compass hove free
in its housing. You slipped
from the cove and were gone.

∘ II ∘

RADICAL FIELD

I

We have tenuous edges.

We have striated hides.

Glandular black ribbons all
inside us,
pelagic and sweet.

We have reservoirs you can't see.

The caribou move
through us beyond
numerous.

One of the cortical
adumbrations,
one of the ferns.

Our heaviest metals accumulate.

We wouldn't dream.

2

Visionary,
the pink sea inches
back where the essences in-fill.

Hard to suffer distillates in the hinges.

Imagine your own bone cells.

Is it an ocean?
Is it this only lonelier?

The bore scrolls in
and delivers its glycerins.

3

Plover sketches over wet
sand ribs.
What you call absolute
groove in the surface,

a trace-sacred.
It's quite certain.

The river's self-effacement in the sea.

No more than this
hopelessness skinned over.

4

Of the dry grasses.

Of the denaturing blaze.

The trans- to all my inactions
or the trance of conflagration?

One never knows which.

The ventricles do open
and shut with such vengeance.

5

What is out-folding here
in the unpoliced recesses

of the dunes?
Excruciating
rumor of a subject matter.

Someone must know what is called for
to be mortal,
to go up close.

The point of return is?
The trend is
toward
branches.

6

Something in the colloquial won't
welcome us wherein
perform the tragical stars.

Part giantess part rust
scuttler in scrub rose bush.

We don't even know in whose influence
we have known it,
the fabled moment
the eye eats up the voice.

7

Each tern just missing
its integer,
each blunt wave
verging on

interstice.

8

How is the ground come up to?
How can it shun?
We knew

we would not be glamorous
but that was something.
That was the old mosaic

interface with somethingness.

What we stood out against.

9

Is it indecent to be broken
off from the birds?
To be oblique and/or
violently finished up?
Is this our crime?
To want abandonment

in the upper mansions?
Are you the beautiful?
Are you the good news
tumor just ripening?

The tough gulls go grim
about it,
the syndicate
streams out-blossoming.

How it all goes on ruining
through winter.
Ruining
and singing.

II

You come upon it vestigial,
onionous,
the blued tissues exuding.

So what can be spared of the nerves?

The orchid thrives on its loveless foot.
The inward earthworm unminds.

Something in the chemicals
remembering

sunlight scumbled over
water,
those bloodroots of cloud.

We grow modern without
being solved.
Fogged in thinking

we are really not this dead, are we?
But gauded with the trick
circuitries of the storm.

We are not waiting?

We are waiting?

We are the red studio?

We come just before the math?

13

All my material
idea.
What light is

like this?
What steppe this
vertical?

∘ III ∘

The Sky Is the Lost Orpheum

The shelter of it carved, caved
Across the river, the park and the little Ferris wheel
        closed down
The great oaks emptying, russet, gusseted
the hovering slant light leaking from the outer edge
        of cloud bed
leads and shawls pulled forth
The synchrony of the lost elements recovered
the shivering water surfaces, planar unmeldings, remeldings,
        riverine alchemies, unlocketed selves
now the reemergence, the sun pouring global gold
        uptilted, gobleted, incanted
Am I not as God made me but stranger?
Made stranger still by what I have seen
at this hour of earth untended, unministered —
light caught up in the river's grooved tread
That sun more like a mass grope out of emptiness
        and the black river weeds before it, torn and trained,
        rocketed and stark and stuck-to
The tall shadow of the willow grows forth
And the spare stems of the grasses and the rods of the mullein
And these are the stations of this river
The houses and the boats and the parked cars
The growing wedge the ducks make moving forward, the shape
        of the element there among the weeds that jut forward,

the mass of the willows growing deeper in green and sundering
The backfall of sun going downward
The surface of the river coming clear of its own admixture
The ducks moving over like slow planes in formation,
        barely seen needles hauling white threads,
        secretly heeding
The fish in my skin relinquishes
Will I know then what I have become?
The river darkens from its end of trees closing in
There is the sun and this deep depression
Exiting as viewed in this river

Gray Shadings

Barely discerned clouds
Hard, hard to get here
what worth, what worth
River of steel.
River of no one becoming you.
Trees that are emptier today, more forced in their forms
To focus on them is to be made glad of them in their
       strangeness
The earth extrudes through them toward emptiness
The few elms dismembering
The willow's bloom above shore like a curtaining
To focus on it is to be mostly taken into its tapes
       and its filters
It is lost to the surface of this river
The dull, impenetrable, intractable surface
resisting, unetchable
Now the faint rain.
I don't know what to do with all this waiting
things getting themselves readied toward emptiness
The scratchy, shattering elm, its crimped skin, its
       exfoliating, its rivening
       its being disfigured by fortune
       and by wind
A crone with old frills at her hair
The grasp of her toward me

Scratchings among the Burnings

clouds in rafts above, upon one another, pushed up along
    the margin of sky
    dark underbellies
Shirring of grasses and the nearly empty apple tree behind
Where is this beginning from?
The roll of clouds bolsters up close
    moves vaguely east
Hear the interstate, its rush of backdrop constant
Oh those deep colors are something sacred
There are patches of olive green, chartreuse, umber, piled
    against each other, snapping and smoking almost
    and then the empty prongs and systems
    cross-hatchings
    against the grays, burnished and glowing
The cloud roll has changed now, been buffeted slowly
    into bunches, disorganizing
Oh, these torches before me that seem to burn brighter
    as the light fades
This aching gradation, smear and
    gleam-forth and then the bare black hands up through
    splaying and forcing the crowns
    so slightly, just a tender worrying up from inside
    the swollen gloves, the spheres of them, the undoing
    the serial falling-off

Furious brocade, yes, devastation
That one oak in its torque
and above, against the maddening subtle surface of the sky
    the barely defined roads upon it, the passages
    the growings-forth
    gobbed and wrought, rich impasto
    stubborn, unbecoming
Now the grays, almost purple, seem to move forward
    branching up from out of the background
    darkening forth
    surge from within the mass
    organisms coming up against each other, bulging and turning
    off, roiling
    slow and mesmeric
    the contained motion of it rooted
    static movement, within stasis
    painstaking
    damage then recovery, damage then recovery
A lighter band of sky now, stratum between dark cloud and
    complicated span of tree-frieze
    layering, up-changing
    free-needled, built-up duns and copperings
    score and rose-green gore, stitch and fret
    always upon the under-thing, the broad backing up over
    the one

Disseminate Birds over Water

The reservoir churned and cloud-deformed
The far line of hills, fused, bunched color
bitter wind against this hunch
my folded bones
I can see the rust earth beneath trees, the rough mats
    gathering weight in semi-darkness, dim
    nesting bases of trees
Graft of dark cloud upon lighter one behind, building up
    of something, a thickening, deposit of cold air, dark web
    of insistence, built up in me
How long can it be here?
A simmering of trees, a dark moiling
    a winter weight
    a mid-shimmering of heat-distorted things
The positioning of bolts of deep orange, gold-green and amber
    molded, wicked in together
Drops in pressure, now, a field of cold, a shift
    between rain and snow
The movement into this remembering
    of separate things, train sounding its horn, removing
    itself from the scene
Snow thickening the far bars of trees, graying them in
Blotting, dulling, gauzing over this dream

It is snowfalling, it is beauty-filling and cleansing
    this burn of words
    it is delivering something seeming to uplift and to begin
    pressing downward, this ink into frozen droplet
    this thing

Snow plinking in the leaves, the left hands of trees
    the neat levers and pulls
    the odd weeds
The rich fringe of emptying trees
    the shifted pins
the breaks into dense pines into period reeds into gutterings
What happens to the opposite shore
    is untenable
    is unmanageable to me
That stratagem of damage, that unmattering
Believe me it is some abomination of things being killed and
    that mattering to me
That exquisite built thing that is obliterated
    its tiny white amplitude, its singing crushed into
    particles, its must on the undersides of leaves
Now I am sure
    the world has not unfolded before me
    anymore but has closed into rows
    of its foldings

Something in the collections of those trees
        bare branches upthrust, the brush of them
        bare branches up-brushed
        their lip along mesh of shore weeds, the flanged grasses
        the scrim of their midst
        I am in them again
        meddling in darks that are in them
        and the white gold that is their outermost
        screen that is their leafleting their grief that is in me
        thin dredge of pebbles and
        strange glandular patternings of trees
        against trees against cut-bank against breath

The rubied lung of sumac
        tragedian

Fish Rises, Dark Brown Muscle Turns Over

rings diminish, duck reflects flight then threads off
Long branch of land, rusted oaks smoldering
    fawn shore, grasses bare scripts of green
    black fingerbones of the willows, splayed
    rubric fringe of the reeds at the edge of water
The reflection is its own blurred dream
The blended edges, furred thing
tawny path of stalks brushed into gray slope behind
Bright yellow mostly gone now, the dominance
    of dulled bronze, ochrous, ferrous grooves of
    the several oaks
The wrought planes and hinges of things
Strange, held-off symmetry, axis of waterline
    rubbed, smeared, edge-shifted
What is real then made more so through
    an intervention of element
The chipmunk's tail jerks in synch with its mouth-pops
Stares hard at me from a dead willow stump
Who are you and what have you done?
Things moving in the leaves behind me.
Dog barks from far across fields
Single bird oars across lake
The sky deep in: dark oxygens
crimp of leaf edging in dried weed stalk

miniature seedpods held forward
calligraphic against gray water, white stones
chipmunk-rustle, upturn duff, chirp storm whirl off, hold still
    hold still
Gravity picks and fidgets

How each blade and bract is angled just so
    arches, etched kerns
    scroll of deft beech leaf
    Baroque script of dried vines
    their wall of texture coming down
Crows burr into woods
fish plinks through and slacks under
ducks quilt across sky, through sky-water
mottled beads hovering, unchaining
Reflection is a real thing set
    in perpetual motion, as if electron
    spinning and jittering made visible
    the static progressions
The waving laminations of white stone
the wandering rift through
the pulse-veins
Breathing thing, made to breathe, graven so

Now the delicate hammers
pure cuts of bird
steel rings reassembling

Quit path under oak
Something moves off a dark road
Deep-embroidered quiet
the tickets slip
thicket in
meter-tick of duck taking off
     keep close, brush close to surface
     furl between bird and mirror-bird
I am vested in sensation
a suspension of yellow maple amid stalks of oak
     distillate of leaves
     saffron particulate
Deep sea of trees, fanned tops of oak corals, collective bend
fast tappers high up
flapping across water
back up the damp trough
trees closing in
two deer pick across, turn back
     clatter through woods
     encircling

Wind Thumbs through Woods

slant hand of beech leaves
shag of oaks before water
When did you go missing from me?
That passage between limb and slipped skin
gouged hickories, the ermine-bright birch
through all that is traveling slopeward
     circleting leaf through branch weave
     corymbs of curled leaves
     lone cedar document rising
Through trees that far land moves descant
the old rusts and pastes undershined
Don't you ever think this is so strange?
the sibilant drift of dried leaves
the coming down all to some shambles
the encroachments on the innermost things
Don't you feel how everything is strained beyond
     certain remembering?
The limbs break their fragile whisks into
The sky is a shroud pulled up over
Each leaf of the beech has its wisdom held fast
its little death ship
I cannot wake up from inside
     this burrow into fundaments of leaves

The cold drills down into the stone
the almost-extracted green
the bird cloaked up under the ribs
the dull gleams

Threshed Blue, Cardings, Dim Tonsils

stripped batting of cloud
glimpsed ligaments
dusk coming up under
lithographic, nib-hatchings
    instruments click
    the fine-sprung locust
    replicate dinge along hill-lines
    tailings of umber, the rust smudge
There is still that hemmed ocean of oaks
    the various reds, the somehow
    silver cast over the brown-gold
    the under-brushed shadows
How can there be more of their dispensing
    into air?
The night-openings of the trees
The thousand clefts into
Their corridors shiver and merge and piece apart
There is no one beside what was once river
Only the carbons incoming
    accreting in leaves
Love of old oaks unencumbering
Root-beauties brought through
crude sieves of bare trees
the few fastened leaves

Those pods are like tongues or like sickles
The blades have been pulled from their sheaths
The backs of the clouds now upturned
They herd from pink seas
They make their untouchable stream
         through regions of steep emptiness
         against which the trees have their gestures
Drop down, drop down toward me
your little sleek scars
Make your bed in rough cedars
clangor of darks numbering in
clusters of trunks and spoked lungs
the thistles that work at the gums

Gold Rivulet Weave, Gauded

chains of the willow, desolate weft
birds and the slim reprieves
the socketing together of weeds before water
straight-pins of jet
incontrovertible smears of dense cloud
      against bullet-train whitenings, unleashed
the reductions to tense
the awful dozes into deep sinks
flush grows upward, secreting, soaking through
      the old damasks
fretwork of trees, their balances achieved
      then slipped off
touched-up surge of cloud across water
The river shuttles onward, reconstituting
It gains the red threads of taillights
the spare greens and the thousand paired whites
      warping over, shaping off
The ducks come forth out of something unclear
The trees drain their weights into water
The ducks are a tension I have not known of
How they pivot, disfiguring the whole field
dragging their trapezoid blear
They are careful and meet their trains behind them like brides

Now the whistles of those taken to air
The disturbance of them in this river
    and the wavering cardiographies
    up-rushed, up-stayed
This is the push of all strayed things into night
the heavying of trees against sky-fire
    stolen into a river, cloistered down
I do not want anything more than this taking
    of last light into pocketings and loose garments
    unbearable closets of the trees
    the stitched-in bones and the placketings
This feeling of everything unhanded
    suddenly let go into robes
The half-bustled willow rails forward
The still surface. The quieted surface.
The same sharp planets exacting there

。 I V 。

ONTOGENY

o o o

You and I emerge
under clouds as to

touch them the least
wrinkle down there is

the groin of two brooks
you have said just

remembering
the bird in the blood

lets go of its ground
the mineral

words store their dangers
so trouble can be

borne off the bones
so a wilderness

room can be got to

o o o

Always the sumac
antlering out of

stones or a path through
woods to a quarry

whose walls lean into
rain whose waters are

the one allotment
in which the fool can

become herself here
is the nubbed tongue

here the lobe end
of the throat you are

like her not in the least
due to everything

you broke in upon
the whole shadow corpus

o o o

Rain in the ground
its furrowing

down here we are
twin riverbeds

one intricate
gilt one soot root

untangling how
perfectly worked

is homeliness
is all you must do

ask to be touched
will something hold

among boulders
will some bird talk

of no high place
you can name

o o o

In lilacs is reason gone
vegetal gone

traceless as light leaving
heat in the scalp

fog wants its coastline so
wholly and so forth

go the murders
on old shale the congress

can't turn away from
the ocean a locked office

you can see inside
the narrative around pain

o o o

Wind in bare vines
rifling the flowerpot

someone extracted
the shattered pine from

the tulips thrust
standards out of walnut

trash and what now
crazes the gardenside

elms a neighborhood
you come to starved

animal standing
shy at the door I

wish for this
world I did not welcome

o o o

Morning its
ridership leaves

each a character
we were not

waiting on
the sun's cropping

up its body
ignescent teeth

of the willow
how

is it I
stand to go

o o o

Snow founders under

us the imbricate

aspen out-shudder and then

the sifting down we do

not fault ourselves

apart I know

you scarce as the seam

between two fields from

just this

far a jet raveling

○ ○ ○

Those thermal bursts

of cloud touching snow

orchard of burned pines

everywhere we are

here is earthly

and winter-borne

the smallest buffalo

exits the iced creek

tinseling and then some

joy I can't intend

o o o

The river muds slump
through alder mesh and you and

I for once stop wanting
what we can't know

downstream between the drifter
heron and the luckless

smolt what we can't
wrest the dusk

swallows

o o o

I study you as you
in this antique square

of stone you the violent
phlox outcome

of foundations the
rich lichened

corpse of the kirk was
that you even in

the sad fairgrounds we
had to cross

o o o

The ocean recobbles
the stormed beach we

once strode over
the muscling

bracken-fern
these new-spruced rocks am

I stuck on not
wanting acreage

o o o

The mountain grips
its sheet of dwarf birch

the wind sutures

down the hinge
of the ravine

unstructuring

∘ **V** ∘

THE KEEP

Is this a kind of progress? This slip-bead
morning through which the rains keep
missing only the scarcely illuminated tread
of clover at the heels of swart pines. Sleep
counters me both ways. I fail to advance
in my own precession by the dark
calendar needles. I will not advance
but by the strange calamities that work
as on shallops on calmed water, a slow
going nowhere kind of motion toward
centermost. You are not here. Below
not borne by branches. You are not that bird,
so rigged as to catapult free
as if I'd the will you would change me.

GEOMANTIC

Spruce of the dark
Ontarian orchards,
spoor of the interior,
I emerge into uncalculated
grain shattering at the crown.

As the sky answers
against the watercourse,
so I take my few
exceptions with God.
Nothing so irredeemable
as the robber cowbird,
as the slump of the fisher
unraveling its host.

The great brains of the beeches
divest themselves so sparingly.
I will outstay everything
for the seasonal observance.
Dried silicles, dried bracts
of the impeccable edge work.
Cords of the drainages in ice.
The rose's roadside stigma.

Black tongues massed
at the interstices,
the lone pioneer oak
attends its assemblage of galls.

EVE PIECES

Comeling

Something still in the mangrove tangle
took my fancy. How it hovered under
the lapping there, a rent in the river
I could fit my mystery into.
The sloe and bark of the water, the damsels
stunned by hustlers, the minnows by thugs.
I had to pause before descending.
Stalk and spear, stalk and spear.
Like a night stork, I snipped and plucked
at the mat of weeds, skull of orchid,
shuck of chub. I trained my eye to love
like that, the garden and its twin
disintegration. There was the still
terrible something to begin with.

Furtive

The moorhen flicks her forehead flame in reeds.
I draw nearer on my raft.
She cannot move with fear
but only lets the long, not plaintive call
totter from the darkened cove of her breast.
And I'd thought it was sudden weather or a drowned
angel come in likeness too close to recognize.

Matter

Could I have wanted anything more
than his secrecy? That sacristy of river
going graces, needle rush and maiden
cane and rack of banyan.
There he offered his procedure:
the bill's scalpel-like intrusions,
the quaking jewel weeds, the seized
and extricated matter. In the cloak
of spare bones, in all the shades of him,
a shelter, grave. I should have stayed,
unfolding only just too much and suffering.

Loomed

Your rouged buds untroubling the showerhouse
wall, it took me so long to know you.
Nothing was changed by discretion.
Someone reached and a world broke forth.
At once, you seemed loomed
from light, your gloves of seeds a universe.
The morning swam and I descended
from you, unladylike.

Undone

Trouble, sprung from the wish I spoke
from between the hawthorn and the bone
white apple boughs, braced like a harrow,
many-bladed, against the earth —
was that heaven? — that tourniquet of hands
and lips and dressed thorns?

Ruin

Dread tells its tale of the orchard.
Seeds stuffed back in the earth.
Like a sheaf of struck match tips.
Of the cliques of honeysuckle.
Pinched to the far wrong side of pleasure.
What this can feel like.

Spurge

The wasp at the fig's chaste inner ear hovers
in the blunt conclusions of the moribund.
Again, I had not lived a long time
and only in upstanding company —
I did not need my demon for a backbone,
just the encroaching hammocks,
the burdocks and the spurge of dreaming.

Salvage

I would fit my back to slash pine bank
and the shelves of reeds, lengthwise
and in order to withstand by lying
down, the passion lofts unstrung, the dark
dragoning the furniture of dead
cabbage palms . . . It was there I seasoned
over. No aftermath but the turned
coves. No god but the one to gather by.

Familiar

Coiled against the creeper net,
his wings outstretched to dry
the distillates of tannic
river bracken and taint
of bulrush: from here I watched
him weave against the lotus strew,
zeroing the bodkin of his bill
with neat design. My confidence
man. My cutthroat. I thought
of the long indifferences.

Tributary

I had perhaps misread the wreckage
of the needles falling, the disordered
rusts repealing the swamp
flag regions and the glade ways
exchanged for dry ways to their source.
Had I not been its keeper? Its lover
through? Its one. Intractable.

Creation

No one to mourn but the salamander
from her bed of leaves, in her corset
of damp tulle, fidgeting along the wrack.
So begins the hard extrusion of again
beginning, the soils that send up tongues
and the acts that stay them.
I was never to be that figure, safe
but braced at the scenes of desire,
in her tears of lime, in her own best gown.

Girl in Me

The moon's old feints at umbrage, the live
oaks' cant and hinge to river's edge
and all loose things damnable in their tracks.
And was I lost to the bosks too long for pardon?
In time, the lawns seemed priceless, the favored
inches of them, the sheer avenues
of trust in them, the drug awns forever
dispensed in a cropped space. And if I'd been made
to grow without conversion, this girl in me
laid out? Oh soft-napped, yielded parsonage.

Coda

I existed.
I knew myself to falter
and from that waste derived
remembering. I set my weir
in a dusk marsh, figuring
the slim pass between good
and untenable.
None but the cattle birds
to judge this a progress.
How one fixes one's own skin.
How a day drops lost
as a smeared kerchief in dark reaches.
How these mullet charge for a trap's
mouth and the shier ones list
in the shallows, tokens of what.

SLOW WATER PRIMER

How to twine the withes
into the casket.

Love could wrest
you in the midden.
Raise your head.

Low among the grasses how
the marsh shunts under
each September, the rich
cement of lengths builds
where light abandons matter.

CARNAC

The thousand stones of Kermario
drift toward their east of cornfields.

Whose catechisms upstood them?
Whose hands whole-mastered the delicate

chisels in the rooms of the dead?
Between wants the mulberries flame

around their quills, each an opulence.
Between this and the being asked of,

kern my unmanageable bones.
I'd sooner know the fires of the old

world than settle to a country of gorse.
Let the good I am bide a bit longer.

KUHL HOUSE POETS

Bin Ramke
Airs, Waters, Places

Cole Swensen
Such Rich Hour

Emily Wilson
The Keep